Cows
Down on the Farm Series
Book 2

MW01152748

ISBN

Published by Little Darlings Publishing

Target Age: 4-8

For other books written by Jennifer Reed visit **www.jennifer-reed.com**
Check out Jennifer's books about farm animals:
Sheep, Book 1 in the Down on the Farm series
Chickens, Book 3 in the Down on the Farm series
Pigs, Book 4 in the Down on the Farm series
Time for a Trim! Farm animals don't want to get a haircut!

There are around 1.5 billion cows in the world. Most cows live on farms. Some are *domesticated*, meaning they live on a farm or are tame. Some are wild. There are 800 breeds of cattle around the world.

Cows are where we get milk, cheese, and beef to eat. There are dairy farms and there are farms where cows are raised for meat.

Cattle is another name for cows.

Cows were domesticated about 10,000 years ago. People in Asia, the Middle East and Africa farmed cattle for their milk and meat.

Cows are members of the *bovine* family. Other members of this family include sheep, goats, buffalo and antelopes.

A group of cows is called a *herd*.

A male cow is called a bull or steer. They are large animals and weigh up to 2400 pounds.

Photo credit: Ross Farm, Nova Scotia.

A female cow is called a cow. An average dairy cow weighs about 1200 pounds. Dairy cows are always female.

A baby cow is called a *calf*. A young female cow is called a *heifer*.

Cows like to eat grass, hay and grain. They spend about six hours a day eating. Then they spend another eight hours a day chewing their *cud*. Cud is food that comes up from the cow's stomach to the mouth to be chewed a second time. Sheep and camels also chew their cud.

Cows have one stomach but four digestive chambers. Animals that have this are called *ruminants*. The *rumen* is the first chamber. The reticulum, omasum and abomasum are the other three chambers.

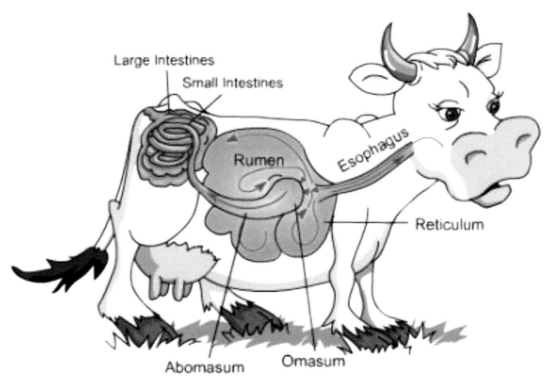

Large Intestines

Small Intestines

Rumen

Esophagus

Reticulum

Abomasum

Omasum

4 Chamber Stomach of a Ruminant

©RoarOfWolverine.com

This cow is chewing its *cud*, even though it looks like it's smiling!

One cow drinks a bathtub full of water a day. It needs a lot of water to help digest its food.

Why do cows stick their tongues up their noses? As gross as it may seem, there is a good reason!

The cows' nostrils creates a lot of mucus. This mucus is filled with bacteria that can make the cow sick. Because the cow can't blow its nose with a tissue, it uses its tongue to clean up!

A cow's tongue is about 12 inches or 30 centimeters long. It's rough like sandpaper.

Cows also have a good sense of smell. They can smell things up to six miles away.

Dairy cows are milked two to three times a day. They produce an average of six to seven gallons of milk. But a dairy cow can only produce milk once she has had a calf.

Cows are of referred to as foster mothers to the human race because they produce most of the milk that people drink.

Dairy cows produce about 125 pounds of saliva a day. That makes for a lot of spit balls!

Cows have hooves. They have two toes on each hoof. They need to have their *hooves* trimmed. It is not always an easy process. A professional hoof trimmer is brought in. It is similar to having your fingernails trimmed and doesn't hurt.

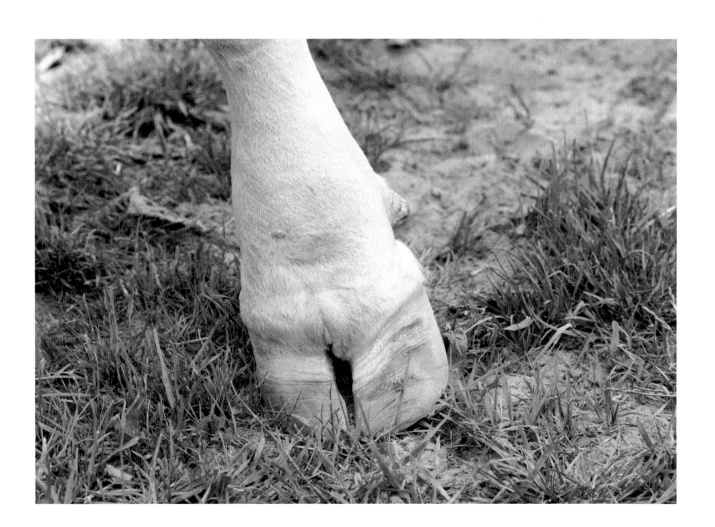

Cows have 32 teeth. However, they do not have front teeth on the top. They have 8 incisors on the bottom front and 6 molars on the top and bottom of each side.

Wild cattle are found all over the world. Water buffalo are from Africa. Bison are found in North America. Gaur is a type of wild cattle that lives in India.

This water buffalo has found an easy way to cool off!

Some cows are considered *rare*. This means there are not many left in the world. Brahman cattle from India.

Belted Galloway originated in Scotland. There are fewer than 10,000 worldwide. Some people call them Oreo cookie cows. Can you tell why?

Pinzauger cattle are from Austria. They are on the *endangered* list. They are mountain cattle. They thrive in harsh conditions like rugged mountains and even arid areas like South Africa.

Dairy cows and beef cows are important to the health and well-being of people. Dairy cows provide milk which can be made into healthy, delicious food like cheese. Many important nutrients come from the milk of cows.

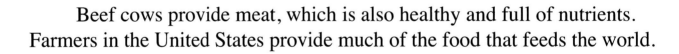

Beef cows provide meat, which is also healthy and full of nutrients. Farmers in the United States provide much of the food that feeds the world.

Words to Know

Bovine
Calf
Cattle
Cud
Dairy
Domesticated
Heifer
Herd
Hooves
Rumen
Ruminants

Silly Cows

Why should you never-ever tell a Cow a secret?
Because it will just go in one ear and out the UDDER.

What is a cow's favorite subject in school?
Mooooooooooosic!

Where do baby cows go for lunch?
To a calf-a tiria!

What do you call a cow in an earthquake?
A milkshake!

What do cows do for entertainment?
Go to moo-vies.

What do cows do online?
They instant moo-ssege each other!

What do you get from a pampered cow?

Spoiled Milk

Word Find

Beef, Bull, Calf, Cattle, Cow, Cud, Dairy, Grass,

Heifer, Herd, Hoof, Milk, Rumen, Steer

```
O U I A H B R V Q W A V R W H W R Z L O
L T W Q G C M W M D P F W B O V U P L K
N Q B H Z H W V N I D E D U O E M B U R
Q J E I N J T Y P M I L K B F S E D B P
O R F L O M K J S L O H Z O E R N M T K
D U I V K G D N O K V V P V J E D C D E
X B D X M L Z U Z S B A F N I H F A I N
S K L I Z D S N D O J H P Z Z I I B U F
J S S A R G U Y H J D L E Q T R Z F L N
S I S V S Q A C O Y G P P I Y N M A F C
C A T T L E G T C R K F K A F R C K Y B
R K F T K Z K R S E D A U M Y E O W R K
I D E Y V N O R E E B N J R B F R J X E
V V V S L I I J D E W O C O X B F J O A
W B A J X V F O A N T A K Y W E B B J I
Q G E V Q B Q C Z V K S V Z L R Z A C R
K X L L W P Y Y S H E J G G T L W K T
O K E O B J D H E H U F Q I S P H F T Q
C J S S I I C C A H H J R D W V E K B L
A X R O V C F P A G D Z P J K P Q R K E
```

64532836R00021